SONGS OF UNSUNG PEOPLE

Songs of Unsung People

FRANK JAMISON

Vista Publishing

Copyright © 2021 by Frank Jamison

All rights reserved. No part of this book may be reproduced in any manner whatsoever without written permission except in the case of brief quotations embodied in critical articles and reviews.

ISBN 9781736877012
First Printing, 2021

Dedication

To the Anam Cara in my life,
the unsung people
who everyday do marvelous things,
and to
the Orr Mountain Writers
for their unwavering encouragement.

"Unsung, the noblest deed will die." - Pindar

Acknowledgments

ACKNOWLEDGMENTS

Grateful acknowledgment is made to the editors of the journals in which these poems or earlier versions first appeared.

In Order of Appearance:

Still: The Journal: "Here Then Is a Landscape" (the Preface poem)
Poem: "Cat Man"
Nimrod Literary Journal: "The View"
riverSedge Journal: "Journal Entry: New Year's Eve"
Big Muddy: In an All Night Diner in Tennessee"
Xanadu: "Last Tango"
Paper Street: "Woman Backlit and Framed in a Doorway"
Confluence: "Film Noir"
Carquinez Poetry Review: "Quilt"
Red Wheelbarrow Literary Magazine: "The Couple"
Fox Cry Review: "Barn on Tennessee HWY 304"
Muddy River Poetry Review: "Riverside Cemetery, Jackson, Tennessee"

CONTENTS

DEDICATION
v
ACKNOWLEDGMENTS
vii
PREFACE
xv

~ ~
Blind
1

~ ~
Ecclesiast
2

~ ~
Metaphysician
4

~ ~
Catman
6

~ ~

The View

7

~ ~

Man with Tatoos

8

~ ~

Bag Woman

10

~ ~

Her Pen

11

~ ~

Unspoken Words

12

~ ~

Journal Entry: New Year's Eve

13

~ ~

In an All Night Diner in Tennessee

14

~ ~

Woman On a Ferry

16

~ ~
Department Store Clerk
18

~ ~
Last Tango
19

~ ~
Postcard from Nanjing
20

~ ~
Unnoticed as She Passes
21

~ ~
Woman Selling Blankets
22

~ ~
Woman Backlit and Framed in a Doorway
24

~ ~
Film Noir
25

~ ~
The Deepest Shade of Red
26

~ ~

Two Fables

27

~ ~

Black Iron Skillet

30

~ ~

Barn on Tennessee Hwy 304

32

~ ~

The Girl in the Blue Tercel

34

~ ~

Quilt

35

~ ~

The Hay Rake

36

~ ~

Riverside Cemetery, Jackson, TN

37

~ ~

Something the Dead Should Do

38

NOTES

39

ABOUT THE AUTHOR
41

Preface

There is in each of us a fragment of the unsung, the discounted as well as the exalted. The people in these poems have illuminated my life. Most are based on actual people I've seen or met although portions of some have come to me in the margins of dreams. The landscape they inhabit is real and ancient and magical and filled with stories.

HERE THEN IS A LANDSCAPE

Mountains worn into hills,
grasses seeking sunlight,
valleys filled with mist like smoke
and a broad river cutting through.
Here then is the place
where hard-scrabble earth
was tilled, flooded, re-tilled
by hard-scrabble people.
Who could have dreamed
luxury would one day be
carved from that dirt,
those stones?

Yet they are not gone,
the eekers-of-bare-living,
into the hard-scrabble earth,
their stones upturned.
Among the mountains worn
into hills, their names still
hang in hollows and coves,
on ridges and roads.
They emerge from the earth,
from springs and streams, names
like Rose, like Laurel, like Crystal
to flow now as they did then,
down creeks and hollows
named Bradshaw and Branham,
Keylon and Poland, from Abel
to Zwicker they understood
how the dead endure as they put
their stories on the landscape:
Hurricane, Dry Fork,
Winchester, Bullet,
Dead Man, Zion.

BLIND

He'd sit there alone in perpetual darkness
showered in sunset and lifting his face
as if certain sooner or later a photon
would find a last living nerve.
He would sense your presence, and ask
about the density of shadows, the shape
of clouds, orbits of bees in the coleus.
He would tell you the number of paces
to the corner at Chester and how many more
if you made all the right turns, climbed
the right steps, 'til you'd find yourself drenched
in the stained glass light of Saint Mary's.

ECCLESIAST

He stands on the corner of Race Street
as clean and neat as a new whistle
speaking in strong commands:

Come, Listen, Hear, Go forth.

He holds his Bible like a talisman
to the cars and trucks that stop
like accidental worshippers
at a drive by altar.

His cardboard sign exhorts truck
after truck after car to repent,
be saved, heaven is nigh it declares.

All fall, all come short of the glory.

Passengers lean forward to look,
drivers glance over at him,
then urge their engines on
as if rising after kneeling.

They see him diminished in the rearview,
but how are they to know whether
they may have brushed the hem
of something larger than themselves?

METAPHYSICIAN

This metaphysician I know
walks slightly stooped, his gaze
slanted down covers the ground.
He sees life at its basest.

Down among the ditched detritus,
the discarded scraps remain
of what once was vital, now tossed off
like old empty beer cans.

You can see him in the early morning
walk the roadsides of our county to get
nowhere in particular he'll tell you,
just to the bottom of things.

I went with him once and tried
to make sense of what was down there,
to read the weeds like him, to see
something other than refuse.

I picked up a snatch of paper that read...
Come see me soon and bring someone,
bring the old broken...
that was all there was.

I turned it front and back,
let it flutter down, then moved on
to look for more of what
this metaphysician I know calls life.

He retrieved the scrap and I watched
him form the words until at the end
he spoke one word out loud,
heart, he said.

CATMAN

Picture this: Watching the show in Key West,
the sun ratcheting down and all around
the complex and the bizarre mingle with ease
as if life should be this way everywhere.
In the throng, one man with his cats
puts on a show extraordinary in its way.
The cats have fine names like Celeste and Shogun,
Cremioux and Babbage and one of them
leaps from pole to pole and finally through fire
before the man takes it in his hands and lifts it
high then brings it slowly down to his face
where he kisses its furry lips with his own.
Everyone claps and claps and the man
puts the cat into its cage and turns to the crowd
whereupon the cat reaches its delicate paw
between the wires, unlatches the door
and leaps again as if to say I will do this
again and the crowd goes wild
clapping for the cat instead of the man
who is bowing deeply.

THE VIEW

The low clouds of a summer evening along the horizon
where the sun sinks like a small grief remembered,
the open deck and two night herons pumping the twilight
beckon the man to the assurance of the railing,
the way an insignificant small craft nudges up to a quay.

His eyes seem to pull the scene from a distance
as if it has belonged to him so long a time it is habitual.
Others soften their talking in the afterglow and he
lifts his glass against the setting sun, the light
through the wine casts a small vermilion stain on his chest.

This could be the arrangement of leave taking, of departure,
or just as likely happiness or recognition that the moment
holds within itself its valediction, the sinking day,
the waters lapping minutely against the shore, the heart
beating the steady articulation of simple pleasures.

MAN WITH TATOOS

He seemed to fluoresce
in the arc of light from the street lamps
as he paced from corner to corner
like a panther in a cage.

He changed from a bluish tint
in the mercury light at one end
to burnished bronze
in the cadmium light at the other.

Blue snakes coiled around his right arm
and red and yellow love
buttered the left, nearest his heart.
He was alive with art.

His tee shirt sleeves were cut away
So you could see
how a trellis of reptiles
snaked over his shoulder.

It made you wonder
what else was there
and how a lover would
handle such a canvas.

Then he stopped and stood
absolutely still as if he knew
what would happen
as the bus drew up.

Its doors opened
and in the new light, he glowed
like a mythical figure,
but his shadow stretched out

tattooless and bland on the pavement,
and he left that part of himself
on the sidewalk when the doors
swished shut behind him.

BAG WOMAN

Look, said the old woman, bags over each arm,
shawl upon shawl, upon shawl on her shoulders.
Look down the canyon of the city where yearning
flows like a river poured from someone's heart.
See how the glass sparkles and glitters like jewelry.
The city is adorned.
Listen. Hear the million pulse beats, made by all
manner of men and women come to find something.
I yearned and I came and I learned this,
she bent a crooked finger and said,
Over there where the real river flows
everything comes to rest in the margin.

HER PEN

for EMJ

I remember the slender shape of it,
its color a marbled green, its golden
tip, and on the end she cradled softly
between her thumb and forefinger a small
white dot, her polished nails glistening as
she wrote and I yearned to have the pen be
mine so I could drift like her across
the page's white expanse and she noticed
my longing. She took my hand and placed the pen
just so and without a word she covered
mine with hers so like dancers together
we went gliding across the papered floor
trailing words behind us like glitter. Oh!
I wanted to go on forever this way,
two step, foxtrot, waltz, drunk on blue ink.

UNSPOKEN WORDS

The restaurant empty, two people alone,
a small round table between them,
his hand on the tablecloth, palm up,
hers against the glistening fabric.
The dregs of wine swirl in the glasses
each one tilts now and then to the light,
an idle act, not a taste of wine
in this patient moment between them.
What invitation waits in those hands?
What unspoken sentences do those eyes
construct between them, what whispered
words? What moments remembered?
There is only his upturned palm, the
fractional movement of her polished
nails against fabric as fingertips
move together and palm rests in palm,
each gazing a moment at something
across the room until their eyes come
to rest on each other to confront
the desperation in those unspoken words.

JOURNAL ENTRY: NEW YEAR'S EVE

They fell together in one hurrah, ignored the ball drop,
the cold of course, the neon glitter.

How far to the end of the year, she asked?

How far away is anything, he asked?

Even now is awhile ago in the physics of it,
the bounce of light, the lag time to the optic nerve,
the brain's registry and yet
how sweet the now and how delicious.

All the old new years are a memory this one drags behind, she said.

Then they fell together, ignored the hurrying hurrahs,
the crowd shouting toward the unknown year.

IN AN ALL NIGHT DINER IN TENNESSEE

He sits neonesque in the lights
facing the counter with his back
to the fogged up plate glass window
as the waitress grows more and more
chatty each hour after midnight.

He watches the cook scrape the grill,
push away the day's detritus.
His cup grows cold and the waitress
says to him, *Hon, let me take that.*
Let me just warm you up, darlin'.

She brings him a fresh cup of coffee,
Here, Sweetheart, this'll be better.

And you wonder how he can be
her hon, her darlin', her sweetheart
when she says that to everyone
who comes in the door even to
those she never has met before.

She wipes up the counter and smiles
seeming to say, *Don't make it so
difficult darlin', we're just an
all night diner in Tennessee.
Everyone's in love or should be.*

WOMAN ON A FERRY

The ferry churns from the wharf
heading for Sausalito, a few passengers
stand on deck in the cold, stand
near the railing, face into the wind.
One slight woman turns her collar
against the chill and city.
You watch her disembark In Sausalito,
walk up the hill where she spends
some time in shops looking, lifting,
asking a question now and then,
her polite smile saying no
not this one, something else.
This could simply be a day trip
from the city, from the cares of a life
or something else, a sought destination
on the spice road, a mission
to acquire, a desire to be satisfied,
a void aching to be filled.
You see her lift two Christmas ornaments,
though it is late summer she admires them,
one a little boy, the other a girl,
on skates, cheeks red, with tiny collars of fur.
She holds them up and you see her say

yes these will do.
Then she walks back to the dock and waits,
facing the city for the next ferry,
nothing else, no other duty, and you wonder
as she boards if she came all this way
to step for a moment outside the complex city
or to plunge forever into her life.

DEPARTMENT STORE CLERK

All evening, back and forth she went
through the racks of clothes
telling the shoppers how nicely the colors
reflected their skin, their hair, how resistant
to wrinkles was this or that fabric.
She caught the essence of each one
like a psychiatrist and their faces
glowed as they flew quickly through
the lightness of things, touching material
and turning as if to say this one matters
but this one does not, evaluating the worth
of each item as she looked on expertly
timing her interjections, because
she knew precisely what mattered.

LAST TANGO

for EMJ

Deftly you stepped onto the floor to face your final partner.
You pressed your palm into death's hand and the two of you
swung around the room, step and glide, dramatic halt,
without the slightest hint of music.
You felt the pressure of his hand against your back, looked
deep into his eyes and knew the step and turn exactly.
You let him guide you to the final flourish and it was over,
applause replaced by silence.
You folded like a petal for one last bow, you didn't even smile,
you simply said *I love you all and thanks for coming to the dance*,
then before we could respond you left the floor,
slipped behind the curtains and you were gone.

POSTCARD FROM NANJING

Looking like two doves anywhere, these two
move about the crumbling quay pausing
now and then as if measuring small distances,
seeing things we cannot, the meager, the scant.

A woman with two pails opens her back door
and comes singing into her garden as she
gives morning water to her squash plants.

The doves leap up on spread wings.

She sees me watching and smiles as if to say
the shift of continents is insufficient
to bring us together, it takes eyes and hands...
that and the great lift of the heart.

The doves circle and settle.
The distances diminish between us.

UNNOTICED AS SHE PASSES

Who says frailty has no sound?
That woman with the walker
shuffling over the carpet
makes such soft scrapings
even she is unaware
how it shouts her condition.
And notice
when she gets to the one spot
where the color and design
shift to a wine shaded square,
she lifts the walker
just a quarter of an inch
no more
and slowly shuffles her feet
over the short extent
sending up such small cries
almost no one notices
the way she has struggled
to keep from making a mark
on the smooth expanse
as she passes.

WOMAN SELLING BLANKETS

The woman in this photograph
drapes a blanket over her shoulder.
With her left hand she tucks it
under her chin and stands
gazing into the distance.
It's for sale, the colors are deep,
vivid, beautiful colors I like,
navy and forest green and wine
with a border rainbow from amber
to fawn woven in, but the blanket
isn't the thing here, not what caught
my eye and made me point the lens,
shooting over and over again,
trying to catch her private moment
against the Andean mist.
She doesn't know I'm watching
from a distance above, can't hear
the shutter's ka-shick-ka-shuck.
So I keep snapping away hoping
to catch her pensive look as she
gazes into, what is it? Distance? Her past?
Or is she simply thinking
of the tourists moving about?

Perhaps she's bored standing, hoping
someone will come, even someone
with a camera draped over his shoulder
to finger her blanket, lift and touch it
to his own face as she does
then smile and offer to buy it.
Or maybe she's only tired of this waiting.
In any case, she is in the moment,
as beautiful as it is, more so
than the blanket, so I snap away,
capturing her forever in this quick,
quiet instance, not knowing
what I will do with the picture later,
just knowing I'll never see this
one beautiful amalgam again
and suddenly it's over
as someone, is it her oldest child,
brings her baby and she's transformed
as she kneels down, hovering
over her infant like an angel
as the blanket lifts and spreads
like brilliant, colorful wings.

WOMAN BACKLIT AND FRAMED IN A DOORWAY

Framed in the doorway she looks like an angel
the way the sunlight makes a halo around her hair.
She leans her shoulder against the frame as if
to take some of the load off and her right hip
is cocked to the side so that she seems posed
for sex or a photograph while outside
the brilliant sunlight fills the scene with heat,
a few birds call and a rumbling train
sounds like the afternoon storm that will build
from the direction where she is looking as if
she is waiting for something to happen, as if
her life is somehow abbreviated but can be
replenished if only it will happen soon and be
something good and not something bad.
Then she straightens herself and runs one hand
through her hair and with the other grasps
her upper arm as if to hold on to herself for just
one more moment before her world changes.

FILM NOIR

When the theater lights come up,
everyone looks around, uncertain
in the sudden return to reality,
embarrassed to be among others
dabbing a small last tear
remembering how the heroine
a few moments ago broke the news
to her lover that it was over,
how the cat lay curled on the floor
at the moment she turned
to walk to the door and how she
paused for a moment in the shadow
to run her fingers over the glove table's
marbled surface in the very hallway
into which they had once tumbled
from the street clinging to the one thing
neither of them ever imagined being
without, it burned with such intensity.
Then suddenly everyone seems to waken
as if from a deep sleep or coma and move
toward the aisles and the long slant
upward toward their lives which may be
remembered in just such a light.

THE DEEPEST SHADE OF RED

After Jack Vettiano's painting: Only the Deepest Red

I thought I'd ask how come you're sitting
here among the framed and frameless paintings,
with your tiny mirror open to reflect your face,
your gloss stick red and perfectly angled
to your upper lip, and how beautifully
your feet tilt into the toes of your white shoes,
the tightness in your calves causing desire
so I am at a loss to explain why something
so animal can exist in me, and yet
you need not move or speak for me to know
I am the alter-portrait outside the frame
in which you sit in window light and shadow
and nothing I do will alter it so I turn
at the door and gaze once more and know
that love can only be the deepest shade of red.

TWO FABLES

I   In the Alley of Dreams

There was this, the fog rising from the water's edge,
little eddies of it like dust between buildings on dry days;
and this too, heel clicks along the walk and leaves
scuttling in the slight breeze and what sounded like a knock
at a door which swung wide and two people
with whispers drifted between them.
And wasn't he the one who said to come, sent the invitation,
said all that about loneliness and absence, sentimental
words in an unscented letter?
A mockingbird sang in the chinaberry tree, snipped
the round fruits and swallowed them whole and all the while
the fog lifted and settled, bathed the little houses
along the shore in light dripped with shadows
and the earth rolled over so that the sun seemed higher
and the little breezes came again at noon.
And wasn't she the one who made the coffee, dark and thick,
poured into porcelain cups with antique silver spoons
set upon saucers and read messages in the cream?
In the afternoon, the breezes between buildings sifted
humps of dust against the walls, between flagstones,
filled the ragged cracks in concrete, and thistle down

lifted and drifted like motes on whatever vagrant
draft sighed from the water's edge between structures
where they sat touching.
And wasn't he the one who felt obliged to speak first, to say
the important words that needed to be said, to say the facts
of the matter in tones much like the breezes outside?
Later there was this, the sun on the horizon, the air still,
the leaves of the Chinaberry tree waiting on a coolness
like the touch of fingers on a fevered forehead,
the evening's moisture from the shore, an embrace,
one last whisper left on the stoop, a door closing,
heel clicks along the walk toward the water's edge.

II The Couple

They were settled in country marked off and divided
by little distances like the thin barbed wires between fields.
It was all so familiar they hardly noticed each other.
When she would come into the room, he sometimes felt
he was seeing an apparition she had become so immaterial.

When he came home in the evening, his voice sounded
to her like someone on the telephone, a stranger
in a cubicle in some far-off crowded city describing
another huge cause, asking her to give, tugging
at heart strings no longer tuned to the old harmony.

Mists on high ridges were no less substantial.
And their conversation was like talking
while focused on a point beyond the shoulder,

seeing other people who seemed to be
conversing in spite of their distances.

One day, she realized she was her own, a nation,
parliament to herself, and he, ambassador from afar.
He likewise, while sitting in his office, listening
to incessant music, understood for the first time
he was being recalled, his tour over, his portfolio failed.

That was the evening they suddenly saw each other
for the first time in a long time, as though they had
each walked out quietly closing the door
with no explanation and no destination then found
themselves back where they began,

like two strangers come together on a corner
in Marrakesh or Maracaibo, sultry piano music flowing
from the open window of a little bar neither of them
had ever noticed before. He smiled. She took a chance.
They went in and fell madly in love.

BLACK IRON SKILLET

Black as night, as black as
say pitch or soot or boot polish.
How black can cold iron get
and still be warm like a quilt
or a fireside or a mother's heart
beating in time to all the dreams
she birthed and nursed just like
they were her own flesh and blood?
The strength of nations in those
arms that held every baby the world
ever saw and stirred every batter ever
poured into a black iron skillet
smoking with heat and fat and some
of those dreams as she mixed and
stirred and sweated over the outcome
like this might be the only chance
she'd ever have to turn out cornbread
golden as sunshine in contrast
to the blackness of the skillet
glowing with heat as she turns
the world's great delicacy onto the plate.

Cornbread and family built
by strong arms and tears
and some dreams shoved away
in the knowledge that she is
the world's solidarity
the world's main hope waiting
like the skillet on top of the stove
for another chance at heat and fire.

BARN ON TENNESSEE HWY 304

Its roof is rust, the doors are gone,
the dimness inside is tangible.
The rustling you hear could be
imagined, a plow horse stamping,
a milk cow lowing, a hinge creak
in the slight alteration of light as when
memories are brought forward.
The wind soughs through the timbers,
and you wonder if it was the barn
you heard say, *I did not bow*
before the wind, the rain, the fire,
I was faithful, I was with you
through the dry seasons,
the wet, the heat, the cold;
or you think it was a denim figure, dim
before the milk cow's stall, whispering,
I came to you each morning
like a worshiper. I was minister to you.
It was I who mended your broken boards,
I carried your splinter.
Mine was the blood on your door.
The wind through the empty stalls
touches your face in the shadowy light

as if to acknowledge your coming
to bear witness to trust, hardship, and toil,
to proclaim the earth gives and the earth reacquires.
Otherwise nothing speaks, nothing moves,
time leans, the waiting is palpable.

THE GIRL IN THE BLUE TERCEL

The young girl in the blue Tercel at the traffic light
tilts her neck and lifts her left arm and with one long
delicate nail scratches her scalp.
The golden stud in her pierced right ear glints
and the few stray hairs on her neck glow as the sun
slants through the window. She rests
her cheekbone on her hand and twines
around her long index finger the hair falling
loose above her cheek. She might be dreaming
about her child or the kiss she gave
to her husband after breakfast or possibly
neither of those things, instead being lost
in a dream waiting for the traffic to move
hoping her life will lighten.

QUILT

She lies down on the cool clean bed
like she did as a child hearing jays in the apple tree,
and she stretches her arms realizing she has
stitched a lifetime from pieces and instants,
and wonders at the whole of it, smiling a little
at the improbability of having been
both inside and outside her time,
craft and craftswoman to her life,
inseparable from the quilt of her time
which folds from her in all directions.
And she remembers how she rose one morning,
smoothed her bed as if to erase the rumpled moments,
and came to the idea that time can't possibly flow,
because it would have passed her by as if she
was simply the observer, watching *it* whereas,
in reality, she made *it* and *it* made her
moment by moment, piece by quilted piece
and her time is her own not someone else's and
it is not possible to lie down
on the bed of someone else's dreams.

THE HAY RAKE

Looking for all the world
like the bones of something prehistoric,
the hay rake sits in a corner of the field,
tines like ribs baking in the sunlight,
fescue and trumpet vine between them,
tires limp on their rims, the air once
breathed into them expired.
This ancient implement stands
useless now, ornament and reminder
to past effort, the farmer's backward look
over hay row trailing behind
the way anyone glancing backward
might see life in so many cut remnants.

RIVERSIDE CEMETERY, JACKSON, TN

What once was a river is now a dry bed
wrapping this cemetery in shadowy arms
of willow and trumpet vine.

Paddlewheel boats once plied toward
the town before canals were dug to drain
the wetlands, taking river and soil away.

I know not a soul resting here,
some marked in statuary and stone,
named and numbered with dates inscribed.

A few mere swales hint of others in the earth,
children beside mothers, mothers beside
husbands beside masons beside tillers of soil,

the known and unknown all come,
one imagines, wondering what happens
to souls with no river to cross?

SOMETHING THE DEAD SHOULD DO

The dead should take everything with them.
  ~ Phillip Schultz, Living in the Past

At the old Pickell cemetery on my morning walk,
a man sat on a stone, hands on his cane.
I stopped a moment to catch my breath.
I was about to say my name, but he turned
his palm up as if to say I know you already.
I stood mute and then he said, *The dead*
should take everything with them. We shouldn't
have to walk among them remembering
the old places, the things we didn't say and do.
He looked over his shoulder at the stones,
shook his head and started down the hill tapping
his cane against the pavement, sending
messages no one answers.

NOTES

1. With the exception of the two poems in "Two Fables" which are strictly the product of dreams and imagination, all of the poems in this collection contain fragments of real people whom I have seen or known though I have fictionalized them all.
2. Riverside Cemetery is a real place in Jackson, TN. The Forked Deer River looped around it once upon a time and thus the name, but during the mid 20th century, the river was channelized to drain surrounding wetlands for farming and ostensibly for flood control. This effort removed the river to the South away from the cemetery. It was this image that got me to wondering "what happens to souls with no river to cross?"
3. The images in the poem "Postcard from Nanjing" derive from a morning I spent beside the Yangtze River in Nanjing, China.
4. I photographed the woman in the poem "Woman Selling Blankets" near Pankara, Peru.

ABOUT THE AUTHOR

Frank Jamison was born in Jackson, Tennessee. He graduated from Union University with majors in Mathematics and English and from the University of Tennessee with a Master's Degree in Mathematics. He began writing poetry and short stories as an undergraduate. He lives and writes beside the Tennessee River in Roane County Tennessee.

Learn more about Frank's writing at http://www.frank-jamisonauthor.com. Follow him on Twitter, Instagram and Facebook.

www.ingramcontent.com/pod-product-compliance
Lightning Source LLC
Chambersburg PA
CBHW062204100526
44589CB00014B/1940